# The Power of the Body, Mind, and Spirit

*Angela,*

*Live your dreams now.*
*Dare to dream...*
*Conceive it in your mind*
*Believe it in your spirit*
*Act on it with your body*
*And it will be yours.*

*Ted Sanders*

# The Power of the Body, Mind, and Spirit

*Seven Keys to Creating the Life You Want Now*

Theodore W. Sanders, Jr.

WestBow
PRESS

Copyright © 2011 Theodore W. Sanders, Jr.

All rights reserved. No part of this book may be used or reproduced by any means, graphic, electronic, or mechanical, including photocopying, recording, taping or by any information storage retrieval system without the written permission of the publisher except in the case of brief quotations embodied in critical articles and reviews.

WestBow Press books may be ordered through booksellers or by contacting:

WestBow Press
A Division of Thomas Nelson
1663 Liberty Drive
Bloomington, IN 47403
www.westbowpress.com
1-(866) 928-1240

Because of the dynamic nature of the Internet, any web addresses or links contained in this book may have changed since publication and may no longer be valid. The views expressed in this work are solely those of the author and do not necessarily reflect the views of the publisher, and the publisher hereby disclaims any responsibility for them.

Certain stock imagery © Thinkstock.
Any people depicted in stock imagery provided by Thinkstock are models, and such images are being used for illustrative purposes only.

ISBN: 978-1-4497-2869-4 (hc)
ISBN: 978-1-4497-2870-0 (sc)
ISBN: 978-1-4497-2871-7 (e)

Library of Congress Control Number: 2011918045

Printed in the United States of America

WestBow Press rev. date: 12/23/2011

*This book is affectionately dedicated to my family who has always been there to support me. To my wife Annie, son, Keanu and daughter, Aaliyah, I say thank you for your love and support. Thanks for believing in me and taking this journey with me. I am fortunate to have each of you in my life. To my deceased grandmother, Momma Ada Smith, who taught me the power of Love for family, I send my prayers of gratitude. To my parents, Rev. Theodore W. Sanders, Sr. and Cora Sanders who dedicated their lives to giving their children the opportunity to excel and realize our full potential, I say thank you for the many sacrifices and gifts of love. You both did a great job. To my sisters, Pauline Poitier, Wanda Starks, Pamela Davis and my brother, Dr. Raymond Sanders I say thanks for your love and support. I treasure the many memories we have made together thus far in our lives. I pray for the creation of many more precious memories to come in the future. I have always been so very proud of each of you. I want to thank the brothers of Beta Sigma Chapter of Omega Psi Phi Fraternity, Inc. for reminding me every day that friendship is truly essential to the soul.*

*I also want to thank God for giving me the opportunity to give life to my voice through the printed pages of this book. I pray that by doing so the lives of many other souls will be touched by the truth of these words. Thank you.*

# Contents

Introduction ........................................................................ ix

PART ONE: Choose to Succeed and Set the Course
    One: Decide What You Want ........................................... 3
    Two: Change What You Do .......................................... 25
    Three: See, Hear, and Feel it Done ............................... 46

PART TWO: Master Yourself and Live Your Dreams Now
    Four: Master Your Body—The Power of Somatics ....... 67
    Five: Master Your Emotions—The Power of Feelings ... 85
    Six: Master Your Beliefs—The Power of Spirituality ..... 99
    Seven: Master Your Mind—The Power of Thinking .. 115

# Introduction

The year was 1989. I wandered down the heavily shaded sidewalk, avoiding cracks in the concrete that hid the roots of the noble oak trees that lined the way. The sky was a brilliant blue and the air was noticeably cooler than normal for south Louisiana in the fall. I remember thinking that this was a special moment in my life as I looked up and noticed the canopies of mature oak trees that nearly formed a tunnel over the road and sidewalk. Time seemed to stop as I slowed my steps and suddenly noticed the beauty of the campus. I had been attending the Louisiana State University School of Veterinary Medicine for almost four years, but I had never really noticed everything that seemed to jump out at me that day. The sweet combination of warmth from the early morning sunlight and a gentle, cool breeze came together with the harmony and precision of a symphony and gave me a deep sense of optimism. It was as if the sun was reminding me of something I had recognized on a few occasions earlier in my life. I remembered reading about this feeling somewhere. The word déjà vu ran across my mind. This unique feeling brought a combination of peaceful excitement and anticipation, coupled with relief and calmness.

I was on my way back to my dorm room from the student union where I had just dropped an application in the mail for a residency program in Laboratory Animal Medicine. The application went to the Medical University of South Carolina with what seemed to be my last hope to land a position in a comparative medicine residency. I had applied to several programs earlier in the year, but to my surprise and disappointment, none of the programs called. This was my second round of applications and, to my knowledge, it was the only other program with an open position. I prayed that this application would be the key to unlock the door to my dreams of becoming a comparative medicine specialist.

I stopped for a moment to pray as I made my way down Highland Road that day. Maybe it was the way the trees seemed to applaud as they swayed in the cool autumn breeze that assured me and gave me a peaceful feeling of serenity. I am convinced that I was feeling the presence of God. In a short but powerful prayer, I asked God to give me the faith I needed to allow him to answer my humble prayer. And at that very moment, I knew my prayer had been answered. I felt my faith that morning—and it was a palpable experience. I knew that I would realize my dream and would be selected to do the residency program at MUSC. I had no doubt. I knew right then that my prayer was as good as answered.

I did receive a call from South Carolina for an interview, and I did win the position in the residency program. Years later, my thoughts took me back to that day. My life's path was determined on campus amongst the oaks. Something special had happened there, and I realized it as it was happening. An unforgettable spiritual moment of hope and faith had flashed before my consciousness. For what seemed like a few fleeting moments, I realized what it felt like to know, without a doubt, that if I asked and believed, my prayers would be answered. I was alone at the time, but I remember wanting to capture the moment somehow. There were no witnesses for me to look to and say, "Did you feel that?"

I tried to record the feeling mentally, emotionally, and spiritually, so I could recall that powerful feeling of faith again in order to recreate it the next time I really needed to have true faith. Recorded feelings are memories and memories are life and power if you believe. Faith, hope, and deep desire are the fuel that allows our prayers to be granted as we have asked. Think of the prayer as if it has already happened and been granted. Then try to recall the feelings you would have at the moment you realize your prayer has been granted just as you have requested. This is the simple but powerful key to faith, belief, and desire.

I thought about how valuable this knowledge would be. How would it change the world if everyone knew and believed that all they really had to do to realize their dreams is believe? All of their dreams, hopes, and desires would come true if they asked and believed. The world of all possibilities for our lives is within our grasp—or, more correctly, within our own minds. This should not be a secret. It is clearly stated in the Bible in several places. The scripture that comes to mind is, "And all things, whatsoever ye shall ask in prayer, believing, ye shall receive" (Matthew 21:22, KJV).

So with this enlightening event, the seeds were sown in my mind and heart. I thought that I should write about this wonderful truth and share its power with others. This book is the manifestation of that truth as it was revealed to me. If you want to learn how to use a workable system that will allow you to create the reality you want for your life and achieve any goal you are truly willing to believe, without doubting, then this book is for you. If you believe, this book will change your life forever.

# Part One:

## Choose to Succeed and Set the Course

———◆———

# One:
# Decide What You Want

Success is a journey not a destination. True and lasting success comes to those who make up their minds to succeed. Success is caused by specific beliefs and certain behaviors that are consistent with those beliefs. Anyone can enjoy success in all aspects of his or her life if he or she understands and practices the rules and laws that govern success and achievement. If you can agree that success is more about the journey and less about the destination, then you should also be able to agree that it is important to set your course. This means once you have decided to be successful, you need to decide what you want. It is so important to have high aspirations. Aim high with your goals and objectives, for there is merit in the saying,

"Shoot for the stars. If you fall short, you may land on the moon." You must actively choose the success you aspire to have. This is a simple task—and it is the key to what will allow you to have, do, or be anything you want as long as you are willing to learn how to use this workable system. I must warn you that this system should only be used to achieve goals that will not hurt others. The system depends on having a good understanding of the universal mind. I'll cover this in more detail later in this book, but I want to emphasize briefly that success and achievement are creative processes and not competitive processes. There is no need to seek to harm others or to gain advantage at the expense of others. In fact, to do so would result in the failure to accomplish your ultimate goals according to the laws that govern success and achievement. These laws work and are in effect all the time—whether you use them for positive results or ignore them and become a victim of your own ignorance.

Like the laws of gravity and aerodynamics, the laws of success and achievement can be harnessed for good if we understand them. We can travel by air quickly and safely by understanding and applying the laws of aerodynamics. For example, if you jump out of a plane without a parachute, you will die when you hit the ground. These laws are neutral and in effect at all times. It is up to us to understand how to use the knowledge of these laws to achieve our goals.

Let me share with you how I first became aware of this powerful idea. I was alone in my dormitory suite in Jones Hall at Southern University in Baton Rouge, Louisiana, when I decided to take a break from studying and rest my tired eyes for a moment. I had been studying for a few hours, and it was late. I remember sitting back in my chair and thinking about something I had recently heard. I could not remember who said it at the time, but I remember hearing that I should commit myself to doing what is right. After thinking about it more, I realized that my older sisters were the ones who inspired me to do my best when I went away to college. In our family, my older sisters were the first to have the opportunity to go to college. They told me that I should decide to do my best and do what I knew I should do to be successful. Although this sounds simple, it is also very powerful advice. My sisters also advised me to structure my classes in such a way during the first semester to ensure that I made all A's. They told me to balance the number of easy courses with difficult courses to almost guarantee a 4.0 GPA that first semester. Doing this would allow me to adjust to college life successfully while starting with a high grade point average. Since I was the only kid in my freshman dorm suite of eight students that was actually studying at the time, I felt that I was doing a pretty good job of doing what I should be doing to be successful.

This was important to me because during the first few weeks of school, I remember hearing that the attrition rate for students was very high and that there was a very good chance that many of my suitemates would not graduate in four to five years. I was determined to survive and even hoped to thrive. Suddenly, a memory from my childhood flashed across my mind and reminded me that I had to choose to succeed in college, just as I chose to succeed for the first time when I was a young boy.

On the first day of school in 1975, all of the boys in the sixth grade at the England Air Force Base Elementary School in Alexandria, Louisiana, were together in physical education class. We were all sitting on the floor of a large carpeted room. Our teacher reminded us of the Most Outstanding Boy Award. This was an award that was given to the most outstanding boy in the entire class for each grade at the school. The boys who received this award—from first grade through sixth grade—had to have great grades, outstanding athletic ability, and good behavior. The award had been won by the same kid in my grade ever since I could remember. I'll refer to him as "Brian" for the purpose of this story. I thought Brian was a great kid because he was smart and a regular home-run hitter on our baseball team. In many ways, I wanted to be like Brian and believed that if I tried, I could make good grades and also be a great athlete. There was no envy in my heart, but there was a quiet confidence that I could also be successful if I really tried.

Our teacher reminded us that we should commit ourselves to trying to win the award and that the first day of school was a good time to start thinking about that goal. I remember thinking that I should try to win the award that year. My teacher really got my attention that day. He mentioned that it was important to set goals and work to accomplish them. He told us that if we aimed high, we would be successful. He also told us that if we aimed for the stars and fell short, we would land on the moon, and that would be a great accomplishment. He reminded us not to let fear of failure or falling short prevent us from setting high goals.

I decided to try to win the award as I gazed up at the corner of the room and said a short prayer, asking God to help me accomplish this goal. This was the first time that I can recall that I challenged myself by setting a long-term goal for achievement. I was not really sure if I could accomplish the goal, but I decided to go for it anyway. I knew that I would have a good chance of winning the award if I gave it my best effort and applied myself. I don't think I had ever really applied myself to a long-term goal before. I realized that there was no guarantee. I also realized that I had to deal with the possibility of being disappointed, despite putting forth my best efforts. This risk did not deter me, but it did cause me to keep my aspirations to myself. At eleven years old, I realized that I could never succeed unless I was willing to risk failure.

It seemed as if months went by before I thought about my commitment again. The idea of winning the award was always in the back of my mind, but it must have been on a subconscious level. I felt that I was doing everything I needed to do to win. I had a quiet confidence and felt good about my chances. My goal was my personal secret. This motivation shaped my behavior the entire year.

On the last day of school, in a ceremony in front of the entire school student body, our PE teacher announced the award winners. He said that the winner in my class was Brian again. I could feel my heart drop with disappointment, but the teacher continued to talk and said that this year, for the first time, there were two winners. Then he called me up onto the stage to receive the award. I was proud to win and share the award with Brian, but more importantly, I was proud because this accomplishment marked the first time I could recall accomplishing a difficult, long-term goal. When I decided to go after the award, I asked God to help me and he did just that. As I walked up to the stage to receive my award, I remembered the day that I had made the commitment, and I knew that something special had just occurred. When I went home that afternoon with the award in hand, I told my mother about my prayer and commitment at the beginning of the school year. That was the first time I mentioned my goal to anyone. That was a great memory that had not crossed my mind for years.

As I sat in my dorm room reminiscing about the glory days of sixth grade, I realized that I was staring at the right corner of the ceiling just as I had done that day back in the sixth grade when I committed myself to try to win the Most Outstanding Boy Award. It was midterm exam time, and I had received my grades. I was pleased to learn that I had several A's and a few B's on my report card. As I stared at the ceiling, I remembered the advice my sisters had given me and I decided to commit myself to making all A's that semester. I knew that it had worked for me in the sixth grade so I would try it again. I said a short prayer to ask God to help me accomplish this goal. I had not received all A's since my grade school days so this was an exciting goal for me. When the semester ended, I was one of only nine or ten students in my freshman class who had achieved a 4.0 grade point average. We all became charter members of the 400 Club. *This thing really works,* I thought. I realized that I had not used this technique for about seven years, but it still worked. It is as easy as deciding what you want, believing with no doubts, and asking for God's help.

I cannot overemphasize the importance of deciding to do well. The power of setting your mind to accomplish a specific task or goal is the first step to activating this powerful technique. Some have even called this technique a law because it works every time if coupled with belief. Whatever you call it, you should know that it does work every time if you believe and act according to that belief. Like the laws of physics, this law works whether we know the law or not. It is up to us to harness the power of this idea and apply it to our lives. The laws of aerodynamics applied to the world before the Wright Brothers made their first flight in 1903. Through their diligence and keen powers of observation, they were able to use these laws to realize their dreams of producing a machine that would allow people to fly. Although human beings had not discovered a way to apply the laws of aerodynamics, all of the flying animals of the world proved that flight was indeed possible. Flying creatures were able to harness the law of aerodynamics and apply it in many different ways to fly. The Wright brothers believed they could fly and their belief helped them make it a reality.

There is a universal law of belief. If you ask and believe, you will receive. Just as the laws of gravity apply to us whether we understand the laws or not, the universal law of belief applies to us whether we realize it or not and whether we believe in it or not. If you decide to jump out of a building, the law of gravity will apply and bring you to the ground whether you know anything about gravity or not. The universal law of belief works the same way. If you understand the law and apply the principles correctly, it will work for you every time. If you don't understand the law and do not apply the principles, the law will still be working, but it will not be working to your advantage.

## The Power of Deciding to Succeed

After President Kennedy decided that the best way to jumpstart the ailing US space program was to help the country to decide to go to the moon, NASA scientists committed themselves to his lofty goal. They were successful in defying gravity and the odds by placing humans on the moon and safely returning them to earth when our technology was so primitive that we really had no business on the moon in the 1960s. The decision to go to the moon was a specific goal with a specific timeline. This degree of specificity allowed the country to do, in space, what it had not been able to do under President Eisenhower's administration. We became the world leader in space technology by deciding to go to the moon. This decision gave the effort a definite purpose that allowed the universal law of belief to take root and grow in the minds of those young scientists at NASA. Likewise, we have to decide where we want to go in life if we want to be successful.

How do you decide what you want? Some people have never really thought about what they really want in specific terms. If asked, they may say happiness, a comfortable life, loved ones, friends, money, and so on. Vague generalities and weak desires are usually stated. Most people have a hard time being specific. Because of negative beliefs, it may be difficult for some people to think in terms of possibilities. To help with this process, I ask people to put their beliefs or doubts aside and to participate in a simple exercise. We will eventually deal with techniques for clearing limiting beliefs. But for now I ask that you consider, in a perfect world, what would you like to have, do, or be? Think big and give no consideration to any limiting factors. It sometimes helps to frame what you want by realizing what you do not want. Then it is just a matter of defining that want in a positive statement.

If, for example, you don't like your job, you should ask yourself what is causing you to dislike your job. It could be that the work is not interesting or does not play to your talents or interest. Maybe the job does not pay well or requires long hours away from our family. Your opportunities for growth may be limited or you may not get along with your boss or co-workers. Whatever the case may be, you only need to define what you do not like about your current job to position yourself to know what you do want in your new job. If you want more opportunities for advancement, you should focus on what specific job you want. If you are a paralegal, your aspiration could be to become a lawyer. Or if you are a technician on a factory production line, your ambition could be to be the foreman on the floor or an engineer for the line. If you are a homemaker, your dream could be to own your own business or become a published author. Knowing what you don't want can help you decide what you do want, but remember to always frame the wants or desires in the form of a positive statement of intention that is occurring now. I'll cover this more when I talk about the power of the mind or what some have referred to as the universal mind. The universal mind has been thought of in many different ways. It has been referred to as the subconscious, the super-conscious, God within us, and universal intelligence. I believe the power of the universal mind is God and I am comfortable thinking of it in this way. If you are not comfortable with the concept of God, you can refer to this intelligence as universal mind or universal intelligence as you please. Basically the mind, universal mind, or God is what is at work in the law of attraction. The law works every time, but there are rules or related laws that we need to understand when we state our wants, desires, and intentions in order to ensure alignment with universal mind.

"Delight thyself also in the Lord; and he shall give thee the desires of thine heart. Commit thy way unto the Lord; trust also in him; and he shall bring it to pass" (Psalms 37:4-5, KJV). This is a powerful truth that deserves our attention. Our brains contain a reticular activating system. This is a part of the brain that is responsible for processing all of the information that we are exposed to and filtering out only that information that we perceive to be important to us at the time. All information that is deemed unimportant at the time will be suppressed and will not be noticed on a conscious level. All sensory information that is deemed important based on what we have programmed into our powerful subconscious minds will rise to the top and receive our attention. The key here is that the reticular system will do this automatically based on our beliefs and programming. The reticular activating system is working all of the time. Have you ever noticed that once you begin shopping for a particular type of car or purchase a particular type of car, you suddenly begin to notice this particular make and model on the road? Before this, you cannot recall seeing any of these cars on the road. Suddenly they are everywhere. This is your reticular activating system at work. Before this vehicle was important to you, your reticular system filtered this information out and you never noticed it. But once you purchased the vehicle, this resulted in a change in your beliefs and programming and now you find that you begin to notice the same make and model vehicle everywhere. Another example would be if you possess beliefs or programming that says that you are a great baseball hitter. When you are at bat, your reticular activating system will rapidly process information and will actively filter out only the information that will help you be a great hitter. Information such as the speed and trajectory of the baseball as it approaches you will surface as the most important information available at the time. Your focus on the ball as it approaches you will be so sharp that you may have the impression that the ball is traveling in slow motion. All other sensory input not important to you at the time, such as background sounds in the ballpark, will fade and you will only be aware of the task at hand. The information filtered out by the reticular activating system will be fed to other parts of your brain to help facilitate the psychosomatic connections that help sharpen your hand-eye coordination and you will be much more likely to hit the ball. But the ability to hit the ball begins with a desire to hit the ball and then the belief that you can actually hit the ball. Your beliefs will attract more of this to you and you will become a great hitter as your confidence and belief grow through practice.

If your belief is that you cannot hit the ball, the same thing will happen in reverse. Your reticular activating system will filter out information that will help make this belief true for you. You will not be able to hit the ball because this is the programming you have given to your reticular activating system. The important take-away message here is to be aware of the power of your mind and your reticular activating system or subconscious at work. Program it with what you have decided you want. Commit your thoughts to this end and you will have it. The programming of the reticular activating system or subconscious mind, your beliefs, and your commitment to these beliefs must all be aligned in order to successfully attract what you want.

Combine all of this with a deep emotional desire and your desires will be attracted to you like a magnet.

In *The Missing Secret,* Joe Vitale outlines the five steps of the attractor factor. His steps are:

1. Know what you do not want

2. Choose what you do want

3. Get clear (remove limiting beliefs)

4. Feel the end result

5. Look for the good in everything that happens to you

Choosing what you want is the key to unlocking the power of attraction. Choosing what you want allows you to focus your thoughts intensely. Focus and clarity of mind sharpens the frequency of mind-generated vibrations and strengthens the power of attraction. This creative process allows us to create what we choose to have, do, or achieve.

## Two: Change What You Do

Once you have a firm understanding of the importance of deciding what you want, it is time to learn how to use this knowledge to actually get what you want. It is essential for you to realize that what you have been getting is a direct result of what you have been doing, thinking, and believing. Whether it has been intentionally or unintentionally, you have been causing the results that you have been experiencing. Your thoughts, actions, beliefs, and feelings have attracted what you are currently getting. If you desire a different life or reality than you are currently experiencing and you have decided, in specific terms, what you want for yourself, then you are ready to learn what to do to make it happen. If you are not getting the results you want and you do not know what to do, this is the chapter for you. You just need to change what you do to get what you want. Getting what you want is not about life being good to you or luck. It is not about who you know or being in the right place at the right time. It is about understanding the laws that govern success and achievement and applying these laws regularly to your life.

In *The Luck Factor: How to Take the Chance Out of Becoming a Success,* Brian Tracy says that the most important life lesson that you will ever learn is the discovery that your main job is to think and talk only about the things that you want and to discipline yourself to refuse to think and talk about the thing that you do not want. To do this, you will need to know what it is that you really want so you can think and talk about these things or circumstances as if they are currently true. He also states that, according to the law of control, we tend to be positive and happy about life to the extent we perceive that we have control over our lives. Conversely, we also tend to be negative and unhappy about life to the extent that we perceive that we are controlled by external factors. The possession of the belief that we are the masters of our fate is a key success factor. So once you realize that you are the master of your fate, the next step is to decide what that fate will be. In essence, you must choose your fate—and then act, think, and speak as if it is true now. This is possible—and it happens whether you consciously realize it or not. It happens whether it is a positive choice or a negative consequence of your ignorance of the power you possess. You can consciously choose the life you want or you can let your faulty thinking limit your success or even disadvantage you with misfortune. Some people say, "With my luck," something undesirable will happen or "Life has been good to me so far." This type of thinking, belief, and expectation becomes a self-fulfilling prophecy. They unknowingly attract misfortune upon themselves with their words and thoughts. The subconscious mind will pick up on this programming and attract misfortune into their lives. When it comes to good fortune, success, or what some have called luck, we get what we expect. We also get what we believe we deserve. Having positive self-esteem is essential. If you need help with your self-esteem, I recommend that you read Jack Canfield's, *Maximum Confidence: 10 Secrets of Extreme Self-Esteem*. This book will enlighten you to the importance of having a great self-esteem.

According to the law of belief, whatever you believe with conviction becomes your reality. If you believe or predict that you will not have good fortune—that is what you will get. The law of attraction will apply and you will attract misfortune. If you believe and predict that you will have good fortune—that is what you will get. Again the power of attraction will apply and you will attract good fortune.

You can assess how well you have been doing in terms of controlling your destiny. You can find out how well you have been using the knowledge of the power of deciding what you want, to actually get what you want. First review what you want in terms of one important aspect of your life. Write it down. It could be your relationships, career, financial situation, etc. Then think about what you are currently getting or experiencing in these areas of your life. Write this down as well. Compare what you want with what you are getting. Any huge discrepancy between what you say you want and what you have could be due to several factors. You may not have been aware of the power of simply deciding what you want in clear, unambiguous detail. Fuzzy general wants and desires do not have power to attract and can limit your results, depending on how vague or specific you were with these thoughts.

Another reason could be that you have a misalignment between what you say you want and what is really important to you. Your true desires naturally align with your values and beliefs. You may want to list what you most value in life to help you sort this out. You should use this exercise to help define what you should change to get the results you truly desire. In other words, change what you do to get what you want. This starts by realizing that you must think differently and act differently to realize a change in what you are attracting to you. Expect the best and that is what you will get. Think about what you want in vivid detail—be specific—and that is what you will get. You need to decide what you really want for yourself. If you have to briefly think about what you do not want to clearly frame what you do want, then do it. If you write down what you do not want, I recommend destroying the note after you define what you do want. This is a good way to symbolically reject those circumstances for you and your life. You should simply practice gently shifting your thoughts to what you want if you find yourself occasionally drifting into thoughts of what you do not want.

When negative thoughts come to mind, I ask people to visualize the negative thoughts as a breath that you exhale. See it as a dark-colored gas similar to smoke. Then immediately visualize yourself breathing in what you do want. See this as a bright pink, sparkling gas or mist that energizes you as you inhale. Pink is a color that represents your heart. Visualize the pink gas or mist going into your mouth and into your heart. You will be symbolically breathing in the desires of your heart. Practice this technique until you can quickly eliminate negative thoughts at will. This is a great way to refocus or center your thoughts in a positive way throughout the day.

You should also change the way you speak about what you want and do not want. Never speak of what to do not want. Also find a way to state what you do want in positive terms. For example, if you are about to embark on a trip and you stop to speak to a friend, remember to choose your words carefully. Do not say that you hope to not have an accident or experience delays or car problems. You should instead say and think that you will have a safe and pleasant trip and arrive at your destination on time and refreshed. You can also state this as a prayer. The way you think and the words you speak are important because they are two parts of the powerful triad that really energizes the law of attraction. The triad is the way you think, the way you act, and the way you feel. If you align all three elements of the triad, you will activate the law of attraction in the most powerful way. Also, if for some reason you fail to align each element of the triad, your results will be limited. It is not good enough to think positively about what you have decided you want, but never take any specific action that indicates that you believe in those thoughts. Likewise, it will do you no good to work late at your job every night because you want to be promoted if you have not decided what specific job you want. And the one element that really powers the law of attractions is the feeling. I'll say more about the different elements that should be considered when you use your thoughts to attract what you want. Important techniques such as seeing, hearing, and feeling the end state are all part of using your thoughts and mind effectively to get what you want. But none of these techniques will be effective if you do not start by deciding what you want.

In *The Secret of the Ages,* Robert Collier states that desire is the first law of gain. He also states, "Whatever you desire wholeheartedly, with singleness of purpose, you can have. But the first and all important essential is to know what this one thing is." We all have a part of us that drives us on to bigger and better things. It is that internal person who is not afraid to aspire to greatness. It is that quiet voice that will not succumb to the limitations that others place on us. Others have called this internal self-ambition or the internal mind. If you have a burning desire to achieve but have realized that the trajectory of your aspirations has fallen short of your expectations, it could be because you are faced with two common limiting practices. The first limiter is not using your whole mind in a certain way. The second limiter is that you are not focusing your thoughts appropriately. First, I'll cover the importance of using the whole mind in a certain way. Then I will cover the importance of focusing on one desire at a time.

We have a conscious mind that we depend on far more than we should. The real power to achieve resides in our subconscious mind. It has been accepted by science that about 10 percent of our ability is controlled by our conscious mind. But ~90 percent of our ability resides in our subconscious or super conscious mind. You will have no limitations if you only learn how to use the most effective part of your mind in the most effective ways. The way to do this is to impress your desires upon your subconscious mind. You can do this by visualizing the desired state in vivid detail. See it, hear it, feel it as you would have it to be.

Convince your subconscious that you have it now. This can be accomplished by using affirmations first thing in the morning, several times throughout the day, and before you go to bed at night. The best affirmations are simple statements that you should write on a flashcard. Keep the card with you and repeat the affirmations frequently. A good affirmation should be personal, specific, brief, start with the words "I am" or "I see myself," be in the present tense, and include action words and words that capture feelings. Also, most good affirmations should end with the words, "Or something better" to allow the creative super conscious the freedom to create an even better reality than you are envisioning. If your desire is to become a vice president at your company, an example of a good affirmation would be, "I am happily and effectively working as a vice president at company X in the AB department, or something better." Another example of a good basic affirmation would be,

"I am happily enjoying my career where everyone who I work with likes and trusts me and is doing everything they can to help me accomplish my goals."

See yourself in the desired state in your imagination. Think about how you would feel and act in that state. Your subconscious mind will not know the difference between reality and what you are envisioning and feeling. Use these and other affirmations to reprogram your subconscious. Repeat these affirmations daily for at least six weeks. Listen to your recorded voice reading your affirmations repeatedly while falling to sleep to maximize and accelerate your results. Once your subconscious mind has absorbed these messages, your super conscious mind will go to work to make it happen. You need not worry about how you will achieve your objective. Just leave it to your super conscious to work out the details.

In *The Great Little Book of Afformations*, Dr. Noah St. John shines a whole new light on the concept of affirmations. He indicates that sometimes affirmations do not work because of our lack of belief. The thinking is that the affirmations may not yield the results we are looking for because we do not believe what we are affirming. To overcome this issue, he proposes using afformations. Afformations are simple questions that we ask ourselves. The human mind or subconscious will try to find an answer for the questions and therefore attract what we desire. The mind has an automatic search function. Once you ask the question consciously, your subconscious will begin to work to find the answer.

The use of traditional affirmations or statements can help reprogram the subconscious if we believe the affirmations. You should try traditional affirmations—if they work for you, then keep using them. But if you are not totally satisfied with your results, you should try afformations. Instead of making a statement that you may not believe, try asking a question that could change your life. Ask the right questions and you will receive. Ask empowering questions. Sit down for ten minutes and write as many empowering questions as your heart will generate for you. Ask yourself questions like, "Why am I so successful?" and, "How did I get promoted to vice president?" Think about what you really want in life and write it in the form of afformations. Then record yourself reading the list. When you practice meditating in the morning right after you wake up or at bedtime as you fall asleep, play the afformations back to yourself. Do this for about six weeks and reflect on the changes that you notice in your life. If you have been disappointed with the results you have been getting with affirmations, try using afformations. I also recommend that you read *The Great Little Book of Afformations* to learn more about the power of afformations.

Whether you use traditional affirmations or afformations, you can use this knowledge to harness the relationship between the subconscious and the super conscious to create. Most people tend to use only their conscious mind to think, create, and attempt to solve problems. By doing this, they are robbing themselves of the use of 90 percent of their brainpower. It makes sense to deploy your entire mind when searching for a creative solution to a problem. Some have discovered the utility of this and frequently review everything they know about a particular problem before they sleep on it. This practice of "sleeping on it" facilitates the deployment of the subconscious mind and eventually the super conscious mind. You should apply this technique to a real problem that you are faced with today. Be sure to keep a notebook close to your bed so you can record all ideas or insights that come to you when you wake up. Then be sure to apply those insights to the problem at hand.

Your subconscious and super conscious minds are your connection to universal intelligence. Universal intelligence holds every solution to every problem. Everything that is—and ever was—came from thoughts. Thoughts are represented by words. It has been written, "In the beginning was the Word, and the Word was with God, and the Word was God. The same was in the beginning with God. All things were made by him; and without him was not anything made that was made" (John 1:1-3, KJV). You can intentionally tap into this the creative power of universal intelligence by using your mind in this certain way. Learn to use the better part of your mind and rely on universal intelligence to guide your thoughts to create the life you desire.

The second reason why your efforts may have fallen short of your expectations could be due to a lack of focus. You may realize that you have always had strong desires, but there are many who have realized much greater success than you have. Why is this? In *Secrets of the Ages,* Robert Collier says that the answer is "because you have not focused your desires into one great dominating desire." Instead, you have many weak or lukewarm desires that are scattered and unfocused to the point that they cancel out one another. To address this problem, you need to focus on one intense desire. It is okay to have many goals and objectives, but you must prioritize your desires and focus on one at a time to truly be effective. Once you have decided which desire will dominate, you must commit to this desire at the expense of all others. Think of your mind and its ability to help you attract and manifest your desires much like a magnifying glass. If you use the glass to focus the sun's rays on one particular spot, it has the power to ignite and start a fire. Unfocused, the light rays will never generate enough heat to start a fire. And so it is with your mind. Learn how to focus the thoughts of your mind on one desire at a time and you will see results.

You simply need to concentrate on it. You may ask, "How can I most effectively concentrate?" You will automatically concentrate on what you most want and what is most important to you. If you want it, you will concentrate on it. This is a way to test whether your desires are truly yours. If you find that your mind is unable to concentrate on what you say you want, you may need to question if this is truly what you want. It could be what you think you should want or what others want for you. In either case, if it is not what you want, you will find it difficult or impossible to concentrate on it. However, you can use certain techniques to sharpen your concentration on your true desires.

To condition your mind to concentrate, I suggest that you meditate for five minutes twice a day for one week. Sit in a quiet place where you will not be disturbed. Relax your entire body by lowering your breath and imagining your body sinking lower and relaxing more and more after each of seven deep exhalations. Then stare at a candle flame. Think only of the flame. Every time your thoughts move to something else, gently say the word flame and refocus on the flame. Do this for one week. During the second week, do the same thing, but think of your highest desire rather than the word flame. This will help you focus your thoughts and activate the law of attraction in a more powerful way for you.

These actions will significantly improve your results because you will have chosen your one great dominating desire, focused on it with your whole mind, and achieved perfect alignment with your thoughts, actions, and feelings. You will be using effective affirmations and powerful visualizations to program your subconscious in a certain way and allow you to tap into universal intelligence. Your reticular activating system will supply your super conscious mind with what it needs to help you achieve your desires.

To practice creative visualization, I recommend that you begin to use creative visualization meditation techniques that can be found in *Creative Visualization Meditations* by Shakti Gawain.

# Three:
# See, Hear, and Feel it Done

An important part of setting the course to the realization of your desires is to reprogram your subconscious and super conscious mind. You must free yourself of all limiting beliefs. Then you need to see yourself in the desired state. You must vividly see yourself experiencing what you want in your mind's eye. See everything just as you would have it to be. Using your imagination to see, hear, and feel the desired state as if it is currently happening is the key. Your imagination and your ability to use creative visualization will be the focus of this chapter. Once you have mastered this essential skill, your ability to attract what you want will be supercharged. Like a child, you will be able to create in your mind the conditions of your life that you desire. Once you have a good working image of what you want, begin to build upon it in your mind. Start with the visual images. Then progress in your mind to the point where the images are playing before you like a movie. Add sounds so that you hear the desired state as well. Once you are comfortable with the movie that is playing in your mind, think about how you will feel at that moment. Pretend that you have your deepest desire. How will you feel? Let yourself feel the fullness of those feelings. This may not be natural for you at first—but with practice, you will improve.

As a child, I used to have the same scary dream several nights a week. I must have been seven or eight years old and I was really afraid of vampires. In the dream, I would find myself running away from a vampire that always seemed to be one step ahead of me no matter how fast

I ran. If I ran around a corner, he was there looking at me. If I entered a room or a building, he would be there waiting for me. It was as if he knew where I was going before I decided to go there. I had this dream so much and was so curious about how the vampire was able to be where I was going before I actually got there that I began to experiment during my dreams. Once I had the awareness that I could experiment with this dream, I realized that this was possible because I was dreaming. I also realized that this was my dream and I could do anything I wanted to do in my dream.

In the first experiment, I figured that if this was my dream, I should be able to fly if I wanted to fly. When the vampire started chasing me, I jumped into the air and started to fly. I was really moving. Much like Superman, I was flying through the air. It felt real and was the most amazing thing I had ever imaged. I left the vampire on the ground and opened up to a whole new awareness of the power of my mind. Soon I was able to outsmart the vampire and physically defeat him. With time, I stopped having that dream and was no longer afraid of vampires. I never had that dream again, but I frequently experimented in my dreams, which became increasingly entertaining over the next few years. I knew I was always in total control of every dream. This knowledge gave me confidence. I looked forward to creating specific dreams each night. I had no idea what I had stumbled upon.

The ability to visualize whatever I wanted was sharpened over a short period of time. I lost this ability to image vividly as I became a teen—most likely due to lack of use. The more you use this technique, the better at it you will become. I used my imagination to entertain myself at bedtime. Unfortunately, I did not realize the power of this ability and did not apply it creatively to create my reality.

I applied it by accident more than as a deliberate act toward the creation or realization of specific goals and desires. The use of creative visualization still worked, but it could have been a much more powerful tool if I had only realized how best to use it to get what I really wanted in life.

I used creative visualization as a high school athlete in Montgomery, Alabama. I attended Robert E. Lee High School and played tailback on the varsity football team in my senior year. I went to a football game at the Campton Bowl and watched Sidney Lanier High School play George Washington Carver High School. I had been working out with one of the Sidney Lanier running backs and knew one of the Carver High running backs. All three of us had an Air Force connection. One of the Lanier running backs had a great game. The Carver running back also had a great game.

Watching the game helped me visualize what I needed to do the following week in my first start against Carver High. All week, I visualized myself breaking tackles and having an outstanding game. I visualized our team winning the game and I saw myself playing a key role in that victory. Every night before I went to sleep, I saw myself running plays, juking, and breaking tackles. I went through different scenarios in my mind until I went to sleep. When game day came around, I played well and was recognized in the Montgomery newspaper as one of three or four players of the week. I had 105 rushing yards from scrimmage, more than 50 kickoff return yards, and two touchdowns—and we won the game. I had successfully used creative visualization with great results. This was a great experience for me as was my experience the prior year.

My first year in the area, I was a junior and decided to play football for the youth center team on the base. There were two United States Air Force bases in Montgomery at that time so they had a combined team call Maxwell Gunter Air Force Base Team. I lived on Gunter Air Station which was across town from Maxwell Air Force Base. Several of my friends on base decided to play for the Maxwell Gunter football team so I decided to join them. I had two close friends on the team. I'll refer to them as Mark and Ken for the purpose of this story.

Mark, one of our quarterbacks, and Ken, one of our tight ends, both lived on Gunter Air Station with me. We also had several players on the team from other parts of town. I also had three other friends on the team who did not live on the base. I'll refer to them as Jim, Roger, and Frank. Jim was a super fast quarterback; Roger was a talented running quarterback and defensive back; and

Frank was a great offensive and defensive end. There were other great players on the team who were also my friends. This was a special team. For the purpose of telling this story, I'll refer to our head coach as Coach Harry. He was a small man who had a lot of passion for the game. Our defensive coordinator was a large and somewhat brusque man who also loved the game.

After losing our season opener 7-0, we went on a winning streak. We had a game scheduled in Pensacola, but the head coach and several of our best players could not attend the game for some reason. So our defensive coordinator served as head coach. I remember hearing the referees talking as they walked through our ranks as we warmed up prior to the game. They commented on how small our team was compared to our opponents—one even addressed me directly.

He said, "Man, you are so small . . . this is going to be a slaughter." He began to laugh with the other referee.

I'll always remember how I felt when he did that and it made me resolve to do everything I could to prove him wrong. I was determined to prove that I would not be limited by what others think of me or their opinions of what I can or cannot do. I decided that I would decide what my capabilities are and never let anyone discourage me with their words and actions.

During the first half, the other team ran the ball up and down the field as they pleased. Their defense was also effective. We ran the wishbone, Power-I, and pro-set offensive formations, but they seemed to be able to stop every play we ran. I remember being horse-collared and thrown into a fence on the sideline on one play. It was not a pretty sight.

At halftime, the assistant coach was visibly upset. After we gathered together in the end zone and took a knee, he started to yell, kick at the air, and pace violently. We were not sure if he would hurt someone because he was so mad. I remember him taking off his baseball cap and throwing it to the ground several times. He could hardly get his words out he was so angry. I remember him almost foaming at the mouth as he spoke. He told us that we were missing several of our best teammates and the head coach.

He also said, "Yes, we are down 14-0 at halftime, but we can still win if we play like a team and believe in one another." He also said that he knew that we were all excited about going to the beach after the game. He reminded us that the trip to the beach and the ride home would not be pleasant if we lost. He told us to look at the opponents and he said that he could not believe that we were letting these guys drag us across the field all day. I looked at my buddies and thought, *we have control and we can win this thing.* I started visualizing us celebrating our victory at the beach after the game and on the bus ride home. I visualized celebrations in the end zone and on the sidelines with my teammates. As we took the field again, I remember thinking that we would win. I really believed we could do it.

The coach called a sweep play to me that had not worked well in the first half. But somehow I broke the tackle of the defensive end that had horse-collared me earlier and I ran for a huge gain. The coach sent in another play. But Mark the quarterback and I agreed to reject that play and to run the sweep again to the opposite side of the field. It worked again for another huge gain. We had found a weakness in their armor.

The coach was so beside himself with anger that I thought he would come out onto the field and body slam us. He called me to the sidelines and told me to call the plays he was sending in. I told him that we were going to run this play to the wide side of the field until they stopped it. He grumbled a bit, but he sent me back onto the field to do just that. On the next play, I broke two tackles and scored. That series, I had three twenty-plus yard runs and would not be denied. We had a huge fullback who seemed to carry their entire defense into the end zone for the two-point conversion.

I scored another touchdown, but we missed the extra point. The score was tied at 14 with only minutes left in the game. We had the ball for what seemed to be our last possession of the game. Mark threw a crossing pass to Ken over the middle deep in our own territory. For the next eighty yards or so, we blocked and watched potential tacklers bounce off of him as if he were made of steel. It looked like almost every defender on the field touched him. He also looked to be out of bounds for a while, but he kept running. I caught up with him and escorted him to the end zone along with Mark. We celebrated in the end zone just as I had imaged at halftime.

The power of visualizing the victory during that pep talk seemed to make all of the difference in the world. I had visualized scoring and the cheers and celebrations in my mind. I felt all of the emotions involved in a come-from-behind victory. I also had a deep desire to make it a fun trip home. I wanted to prove to the referees that they had grossly underestimated our team—and me in particular. I made a point to go up to both referees after the game to shake their hands and say that I did pretty well for a little guy after all.

They both smiled and gave me respect. I clearly saw the victory, heard the sounds associated with that victory, and felt the powerful emotions related to a thrilling victory.

Athletes all over the world realize the power of creative visualization. This technique has enhanced the performance of athletes for years. Others who need to perform also find the use of visualization helpful. The naval aerobatics team, the Blue Angels, practices their entire flight performance sitting at a table together with their eyes closed. The leader gives all of the verbal commands as if they were actually flying and performing the routine. This is a powerful application of visualization of an entire team that enables them to consistently perform at a high level.

I hope to help you maximize your success by teaching you how to use this amazing tool in a certain way that will yield powerful results for you. The most effective times to practice creative visualization are at bedtime and first thing in the morning. Your subconscious will find a way to create what you see in your mind's eye. To begin this exercise, sit down and decide what goal you want to accomplish next. Focus on this goal with singleness of purpose and place all other goals to the side for now. Write this goal down in your personal notebook. Describe it in detail and be brief but specific. For example, a goal could be framed like this. *I am a vice president of operations at my current company or something better.* Then while relaxing with your eyes closed in a quiet place where you will not be disturbed, create the visual pictures that capture this goal. You can visualize yourself being informed that you have just been promoted. See the e-mail announcement drafted by your supervisor. You may even want to draft the note. See your name and title on your new business cards. You can replay how you will react and feel when your friends, family, and colleagues congratulate you on our promotion to vice president of operations. Think about how you will feel and act when you are promoted and let yourself feel those feelings as if they are actually occurring now. See your new paycheck and office. Hear the congratulatory well wishes from the president of the company. Get lost in the visualization and enjoy it. Be thankful and show gratitude for making this a reality now. End the movie in your mind by saying I am the VP of operations at X Corporation or something better, give thanks, and forget about it and go to sleep. There is no need to try to figure out how to make it happen, but be alert to any and all ideas that cross your mind.

Action will be required. Write down all ideas that come to you over the next few days and weeks. Keep your notebook with you at all times. Then take action. Follow through on the inspired ideas that your reticular activating system presents. Universal mind will reveal your action plan, but it will be up to you to do it. Just do it and you will realize your goal. Stay positive, optimistic, and confident that your goal has already been achieved. Take some action that will show your faith in this reality. If you will be able to purchase another car after you are promoted to VP, go look at new cars and clean out the garage to make room for the new car. Any action that shows that you believe will help. Repeat this visualization every morning and evening at bedtime for at least six weeks.

See it, hear it, feel it, be thankful for it, and take some action to show your faith and belief each day. Never doubt it and you will have it. Know that you have it and it will be yours. Ask, seek, and knock. Doubt not and believe. The power of visualization will change your life.

You can apply this powerful tool to long-term and short-term goals. Map out your long-term strategic plan for success. Use vision mapping by creating a poster that contains images of that you want to achieve. Write down affirming statements that capture your desires in positive terms. Read these statements several times per day. Record a narrative in your own voice that describes your feelings and images you imagine you will experience at that moment you realize your goal or desire. Listen to this recording first thing in the morning and when you go to bed at night. Then take one goal at a time and apply this technique of creative visualization to each step or sub-goal. Stay cheerful, positive, and optimistic. Visualize your desired state at least twice daily. See it in vivid color or high-definition, digital quality complete with surround sound. Recreate emotional scenarios associated with your accomplishments. Believe and feel it. If you do this and doubt not, you will accomplish your goals every time. Remember to give thanks and show gratitude daily for your success.

# Part Two:

# Master Yourself and Live Your Dreams Now

# Four: Master Your Body—The Power of Somatics

Most people would agree that the power of the mind plays an important part in our ability to be effective and successful. The idea that says if you think you can do something—or if you think you cannot do something—you will be right in either case, has been accepted by many with the recently popularized ideas of the power of attraction. The power of the mind has been uncovered within the popular culture, but many people have not been exposed to the truth about the power of the body. Connecting with the body in an authentic way enables one to truly be present, grounded in what is important, and centered in a way that is powerful. This chapter will introduce some ideas about the benefits of the awareness of the body or somatics and the many different ways specific body-related practices can improve effectiveness.

Somatics—introduced to me by Richard Strozzi-Heckler at the Strozzi Institute—is a discipline or set of practices that focuses on the body. In *Being Human at Work: Bringing Somatic Intelligence into Your Professional Life*, he says that somatics is a set of practices that produce:

- A centered presence in which we learn to be present to others while staying firmly grounded in what we care about

- The capacity to generate, receive, and repair trust when we break it

- Empathy and respect for others

- The ability to listen

- The knowledge of what it is to be authentic

- The ability to coordinate effectively with others

- The desire to be lifelong learners

I became interested in somatics for the first time after one of my supervisors introduced me and her entire team to somatic practices in an effort to improve our leadership effectiveness. I had a lot of respect for this supervisor—even though I had little experience with her at that time. She mentioned to me that her career really took off shortly after she started practicing somatics. I was always interested in sharpening my leadership skills to aid with career advancement and was curious about how the practice of somatics could help. I was pleased to learn that our entire leadership team was scheduled to have one of our face-to-face meetings at the Strozzi Institute. While there, we learned about centering ourselves and were introduced to several other practices that I have continued to use with success.

In *The Leadership Dojo: Build Your Foundation as an Exemplary Leader,* Richard Strozzi-Heckler describes the process of centering. The benefits of centering and constantly coming back to center are many. In *The Leadership Dojo*, Strozzi-Heckler referred to *Silent Messages* by Albert Mehrabian, professor emeritus of psychology at UCLA. Mehrabian asked, "What makes someone credible?" and "Why do we trust someone?" Studies have shown that almost 90 percent of what makes someone credible is in body expressions rather than the words that are spoken. In other words, what makes us credible has more to do with tone of voice, facial expressions, body posture, position, and movements of the eyes, breathing patterns, volume of voice, hand gestures, and eye contact than the actual words spoken. I recommend that you read chapter six of *The Leadership Dojo* for a thorough treatment of the benefits and principles of centering. For the purpose of offering a brief introduction to the ideas of centering, I focus on how centering can help us to be present. Whether we need to collect ourselves prior to an important business presentation, athletic performance, or courageous conversation, being present will enhance our ability to be authentic and trustworthy. The authenticity that will spring out of a centered state will ensure congruence between our actions, mood, body language, tone of voice, facial expressions, intentions, commitments, and thoughts. This will allow you to build trust with others as well as with yourself.

## Centering Practice

To be present, practice centering your body. We will start by bringing awareness to the three somatic dimensions of width, length, and depth. Aligning our bodies with the natural forces of gravity along these three dimensions puts our physical bodies in harmony with the energy field of the planet or physical world around us. In this state, our bodies will be relaxed and cease all struggles against gravity. This natural relaxed state of being will free our body energy to be present in the moment.

First relax and stand straight up with your arms comfortably down by your sides. Think of the three dimensions of width, length, and depth. Make sure that your head is centered over your shoulders, your shoulders directly over your hips, your hips over your knees, and your knees over the midpoint of your feet. This concept of centering can also be applied in the sitting position. Now that your body is positioned correctly, become aware of the muscles of the face—especially around the eyes and forehead. Relax the jaw and make sure that the teeth are not touching. Relax the neck and shoulder area by raising the shoulders and dropping them once or twice.

In *The Leadership Dojo*, Strozzi-Heckler says, "A natural response to fear is to lift the shoulders, and if we chronically hold our shoulders up, we're inviting the emotion of fear. We may not have anything to be afraid of or even think we're afraid of something, but raised shoulders move us toward a fearful experience of life." So drop and relax your shoulders.

Different people carry tension in different areas of the body. The common areas are the jaw, neck, shoulder, and chest. Another common area for tension is the face—especially the areas around the eyes and forehead. It is a good practice to relax your body from head to toe. Start with relaxing the muscles under your scalp. Then visualize a wave of relaxation moving down your body. Relax the muscles of your face and soften the eyes. Relax the jaw and make sure your teeth do not touch. Visualize the wave moving down our body to the neck and shoulders. Lift the shoulders and drop them twice. When the wave reaches your chest and stomach, take three deep breaths and let your breathing rate drop or slow. Relax the arms and hands and keep your hands open but slightly curved. Then relax your buttocks and pelvic area.

Allow the wave of relaxation to move past the thighs and to the knees. Do not lock the knees. Relax the lower legs, feet, and toes. Then gently touch the area about two inches below the navel. This is the center of your body—touching this area brings your attention to this area. This is your body's center of gravity. Focusing your attention in this area helps to anchor your centered state. Then think about how you feel. What do you notice about your body? Remember this feeling. This will help you to anchor or recognize that you are centered in the future. Also take mental note of your mood. Mood awareness helps to ensure presence in the moment. Reflect on how you feel now—whether you are happy, distracted, excited, or nervous does not really matter. Just drawing your awareness to your mood will help you be present in the moment. This centered and present state will significantly improve your potential for effectiveness with people. It will also improve your personal performance—whether you are performing an athletic act, delivering an important speech, going into a job interview, or doing anything that requires your best effort.

The key to this practice is to get in a habit of centering and re-centering yourself throughout the day. Certain situations may put you off center. Simply come back to center as often as you need to.

To learn more about somatic intelligence, you may want to read *The Leadership Dojo* and *Being Human at Work: Bringing Somatic Intelligence into Your Professional Life* by Strozzi-Heckler. You may also want to read *Body Brilliance: Mastering Your Five Vital Intelligences* by Alan Davidson.

Fasting is another important way to harness the power that comes through mastery of the body. Fasting has a spiritual basis that connects the physical body and the mental will with the spiritual essence of the universe. Since I am a Christian, I will share some key lessons and truths that could lead you to accessing the power of biblical fasting. Although I will be discussing fasting from a Christian perspective, I acknowledge that other religions and beliefs also value and recognize the power of fasting. The application of this knowledge will transform your life. In *Fasting: Opening the Door to a Deeper, More Intimate, and More Powerful Relationship with God*, Jentezen Franklin discusses the power of the threefold cord. In Ecclesiastes 4:12, Solomon pointed out that a cord, or rope, braided with three strands is not easily broken. The three elements are the duties to pray, give, and fast. Each of these duties is powerful, but when combined in the life of a believer, they unleash unusual favor and success.

Matthew 17 speaks of an incident when the disciples, who Jesus had giving the power to cast out evil spirits and to heal diseases, could not cast out demons and cure a boy who had been brought to them. Jesus was able to cast out the demons and cured the boy. Later, the disciples asked Jesus why they were not able to cure the boy and Jesus replied, "Because of your unbelief: for verily I say unto you, If you have faith as a grain of mustard seed, ye shall say unto this mountain, Remove hence to yonder place; and it shall remove; and nothing shall be impossible unto you. Howbeit this kind goeth not out but by prayer and fasting" (Matthew 17:20-21, KJV).

There are several types of fasts to consider: a full or absolute fast, a normal fast, and a partial fast. You should consider which type is best for you and your personal situation. With the full or absolute fast, you would refrain from eating or drinking anything. It goes without saying that this type of fast should only be undertaken after consulting your doctor to make sure it is safe for you. It should also only be sustained for short periods of time.

The other type of fast is the normal fast. In a normal fast, you would not eat anything, but you can drink water. Depending on the duration of the normal fast many have taken in juices or even chicken broth to keep up their energy level.

Another type of fast is a partial fast. A partial fast could take many different forms. It could require you to fast from sunup to sundown. It could also require you to avoid meat, bread, or sweets. Your partial fast could call for you to refrain from drinking particular types of beverages such as alcoholic drinks or sodas or anything other than water. Remember that fasting is a personal act and should not be advertised. Keep your fast to yourself and God will reward you publicly. You should not look or act like you are fasting or hungry. Also remember that if your fast is meaningful to you, it will be meaningful to God and he will hear your prayer. So depriving yourself of something that does not mean anything to you will not be as powerful as depriving yourself of something that you really like or appreciate. It is also important to bear in mind that fasting is not a holy diet. Your fast may result in weight loss, but this is not the purpose of the fast.

After deciding to fast, you must decide on the duration of the fast. It is really up to you, but when I think if fasting, I think of several different intervals of time for the durations. Based on evidence in the Bible, you can fast for one day, three days, seven days, twenty-one days, or forty days. Moses was in a forty-day fast when God gave him the Ten Commandments (Exodus 34:27-28). To save the Jews from destruction, Esther asked all of the Jews in her city to join her in a full fast for three days (Esther 4-7). In *Fasting*, Franklin mentioned that Joshua and Jesus also fasted for forty days, Daniel partially fasted for twenty-one days, Paul fasted for three days and again for fourteen days, and Peter fasted for three days. All of these fasts yielded the desired results of answered prayer.

The bottom line is that there is not a right type or duration of fast for everyone or every situation. The most important thing to do is to get started. I suggest that you start with a partial fast. Eliminate something from your diet for one to three days. Then move on to a full fast for one day at first, then three days. Then you can move on to a full fast from sunup to sundown for three days and eventually for one week. Remember that the power of fasting stems from prayer and prayer is rooted in faith. Fasting is a way to put you in a constant state of prayer.

The other aspect of fasting that struck me as enlightening when I read *Fasting* is that when you fast is also important. He discussed the power of starting the year with a twenty-one-day fast. Franklin is the pastor of Free Chapel in Gainesville, Georgia, and recently Orange County, California. He and his congregation of 10,000 start the year with a twenty-one-day fast. He states that their fasting at the beginning of the year is based on principles that have been adapted from Dr. Bob Roger's *101 Reasons to Fast*. There are three reasons to start the year with a fast. The first is that you set the course for the year by starting off with a fast much as you would be starting your day with a prayer. This is a powerful way to put God first and giving him the first part of the day, the first day of every week, the first portion of every dollar, and the first consideration in every decision.

The second is that blessings will happen for you and your family all year long because you fasted in January. You may not even remember your January fast in August when you receive a promotion and raise. Or when you learn that a loved one is safe after a horrible accident in December. Blessings will come throughout the year. This is like planting the seeds of blessing that you can harvest and enjoy throughout the year.

The third is based on the scripture found in Matthew 6:33: "Seek first the kingdom of God and His righteousness, and all these things shall be added to you."

By starting the year in this way, you will be positioned to receive everything you need throughout the year.

To learn more about the power of fasting, I recommend *101 Reasons to Fast* and *Fasting*, by Bob Rogers.

# Five: Master Your Emotions—The Power of Feelings

The importance of your emotional state cannot be understated. Your feelings or emotional state has a tremendous impact on your body and on your mind. Emotional stress can impact health in profound ways, leading to psychosomatic illness, including headaches, insomnia, muscle tension, and back or neck pain. Emotional stress can impact the body's ability to resist infections. The way we feel can impact our performance at work and our relationships with friends and family. Depression is a problem for millions of people around the world. Life would be better for many people if they could figure out how to better manage their emotional state.

In *Emotional Discipline: The Power to Choose How You Feel, 5 Life-Changing Steps to Feeling Better Every Day*, Charles Manz introduces the concept of self-leadership as, "the overall process and various specific strategies we use to create the motivation and direction we need to cope with and even thrive in our life and work." He focuses on the most potent part of the process—our emotions and feelings. He called the overall process of choosing how we feel, emotional discipline. He describes the five components or steps for practicing emotional discipline:

1. Cause—identify the immediate cause of your emotions.

2. Body—assess the location and intensity of your physical reactions.

3. Mind—identify the thoughts and beliefs that accompany your physical reactions.

4. Spirit—note what part of yourself is being revealed in your response to your current circumstances.

5. Choice—make an emotional discipline choice and apply it for constructively dealing with your immediate challenge.

Manz holds to the belief that the choices we make hold the key to influencing the way we feel. And that the way we feel has a great impact on our effectiveness, energy level, and fulfillment in life. Manz describes strategies for making sensible, healthy choices such as eating right and exercising regularly. These choices sometimes seem to be associated with a tremendous amount of sacrifice and willpower. The practices covered in Manz's book share strategies that approach these choices in a more reasonable way.

The first step is to focus on the cause. To focus on the cause, ask yourself what has happened that has resulted in or triggered emotions for you. Have you been disappointed at home or work? Are you experiencing unfortunate circumstances? In step one, you need to identify what is causing the feelings.

In step two, you need to focus on the body. Pay attention to your body to determine the location of the physical sensation. Depending on the nature of the emotion, the sensation could be pleasant or uncomfortable.

Where do you feel the sensations? When I first started to practice the five steps, the exercise took me back to when I was three or four years old. Every time I became upset, I experienced a painful sensation in my throat, around my Adam's apple. The pain was so pronounced that I complained to my mother about it on multiple occasions. There was no question in my mind at that time—I was definitely aware of the location of that pain. In fact, on several occasions, I felt that the situation that led to the original cause of my emotions was eclipsed by the pain in my throat. The physical manifestation of the emotion was the only thing that I could think of. I soon forgot all about the issue that had triggered the original emotion—I just wanted my throat to stop hurting.

Pleasant emotions can also trigger physical sensations. The first time I experienced what most people would describe as butterflies was in junior high school. I had a crush on a girl that I had met at the fair that came to our base in Lakenheath, England. We rode the merry-go-round about ten times that night and really enjoyed hanging out together. Since she did not go to the same school as I did, I could only see her on the weekends—if I was lucky. One day, I noticed that every time a thought of her crossed my mind, I would be struck with an unusual sensation in my stomach and abdominal area. It felt like a wave of energy that ran from my chest to my abdominal region. The sensation triggered goose pimples all over my body and caused my heart to beat rapidly. This is an example of a pleasant physical sensation that was triggered by feelings.

Another example is the feeling I would get every time I would read a letter from my wife, Annie, prior to getting married. I experienced a light, pleasant sensation around my heart. I also experienced a similar sensation as I approached my parent's home for a visit. Before I met Annie, I used to think that there was no better feeling than the one I got when I went home to visit my Mom and Dad. The excitement could be felt in my chest as a rapid, light heartbeat. I have noticed these pleasant sensations throughout my life and have attempted to recreate the sensations whenever I was in need of an emotionally positive boost. Many times, I was successful, but sometimes I noticed that I could not recreate the feelings. However, even without the knowledge of emotional discipline, I seemed to realize that I could choose to recreate pleasant feelings whenever I wanted to.

In step three, you need to focus on the mind. Pay attention to the thoughts that traverse your mind. Notice any images that accompany these thoughts. Take note of the statements that cross your mind. Seek to discern whether statements such as, "I am having a horrible day" or "I am having a wonderful day" are passing through your mind. Also take note of the mental images or pictures that cross your mind. Seek to discern whether images such as seeing yourself succeeding or failing at a task or sporting event are passing through your mind. Try to identify what beliefs underlie your thoughts. What beliefs do you hold that form the foundation for your mental and physical reactions?

For example, do you believe that anyone who disagrees with you does not like you and is trying to harm you . . . all problems are bad and will turn out badly . . . arguing should be avoided . . . disagreeing with you represents an attack on you. Try to focus on what beliefs may be responsible for your reaction to the situation.

The fourth step is to focus on your spirit. Try to determine what part of your self is being revealed and what part is being hidden. What part of your inner self is actively engaged? For example, in your response to this issue or event, are you acting from a secure state or presence that is grounded in openness and caring with a loving spirit? Or are you acting from an insecure state or presence that is grounded in fear and defensiveness with a spirit of hostility? As you work through this process for different situations, try to notice the different aspects of yourself that you live, act, and react from in different types of situations. You may notice patterns or tendencies in the places your spirit wants to go. You should take mental note of those parts of yourself that you want to be more revealed—and those that you would want to be less revealed.

For example, you could find that when faced with a disagreement, you operate from a defensive state and become fearful and hostile. This may be revealed to you when you decide to quiet your mind and seek to notice. Once you become accustomed to noticing, you can move to a place where you are ready to ask yourself if this part of your response is desirable for you. If it is desirable, ask yourself why. If you decide that it is not desirable, ask yourself why not. Once you have answered these questions to your satisfaction, you can begin to transition your mind and emotions to a position of power by asking yourself what mental or emotional response would be more helpful, productive, and desirable for you.

This leads us to step five—making a choice. In this step, you will choose your emotional response. The power of emotional discipline is in its potential to increase your ability to choose how you feel. It allows you to decide how you would like to respond. If you believe that you can choose the best emotional response for any particular situation, what would you choose? What emotional discipline choices have you built into your repertoire of responses? Your goal should be to use the information that you have learned in steps 1-4 to help you choose the most productive, positive, and empowering emotional response for the situation at hand. I would like to acknowledge that these five steps of emotional discipline represent my attempt to summarize my understanding of Manz's work and ideas in *Emotional Discipline: The Power to Choose How You Feel, 5 Life Changing Steps to Feeling Better Every Day.* I highly recommend that you read this book to learn more about emotional discipline.

With emotional discipline, you will move to an exciting—and very different—paradigm. This important idea will allow you to transcend the victim mindset and take control of your emotions. With emotional discipline, we move from feeling a certain way based on an experience with our external world or circumstances to deciding how we want to feel after reflecting on—and truly appreciating—what we initially feel. The idea that we can control how we feel by choosing the feelings we prefer is a powerful one.

It is not possible for anyone to make you feel sad or angry. It is also not possible for anyone to make you feel happy or appreciated. It is true that someone can say something that could be interpreted as insulting. Or they could treat you in a way that could be interpreted as being disrespectful. But you need not feel that way unless you decide to open yourself up to experiencing those unpleasant feelings. It is true that when faced with unpleasant circumstances, the truly enlightened person will seek to feel in a way that is most productive and positive for them. Most people would agree that it is to their advantage mentally, emotional, physically, and spiritually to feel happy and good about themselves, but most people choose to do just the opposite. Thousands of people go through life suffering mentally, emotionally, physically, and spiritually because they have failed to learn what you have just been introduced to. *You have the power to choose how you feel. And the way you feel or your emotional state has a huge impact on your well-being, effectiveness, health, relationships, performance, and overall fulfillment and success in life.* These emotional factors or choices influence your success in life in many ways and you have just learned that you can choose them regardless of what circumstances you may be faced with. Your challenge is to start to practice this new discipline and make it a part of your daily life of successful practices and beliefs.

When I think of how best to benefit from practicing the five-step process for emotional discipline, I see a parallel between centering the body and deciding how to feel to best deal with the challenges of the day. To ensure peak performance, it is important to operate from a centered state with respect to the body. It is also important to maintain emotional balance to ensure peak performance. As we work to increasingly become aware of our bodies and moods as a part of practicing the discipline of somatics, we should also become more aware of our feelings and seek a balanced state emotionally by using the five-step process to most effectively respond to the challenges we face on a daily basis.

# Six: Master Your Beliefs—The Power of Spirituality

Mastering your beliefs is about knowing what you believe. True authenticity is not possible without grounding ourselves in what we believe. This is true whether you believe in a higher power or not. I believe in God and Jesus Christ. I was raised as a Christian and strive to live my life according to this faith. I view the world and my experiences through the lens of my spiritual beliefs. I realize that there are other religions and other beliefs. The purpose of this chapter is not to validate one religious belief over another, but rather to point out the importance of being sincerely grounded in the beliefs and higher power you have been led to.

To some, humans are mortal beings that occasionally have spiritual experiences. But many enlightened people, including myself, believe that humans are spiritual beings who are temporarily having a mortal experience called life. To truly be effective, we must recognize all aspects of our existence. We are multi-dimensional beings with a body, mind, emotions, and a spirit. We need to nurture and attend to each aspect of ourselves to reach our full potential.

There are many different ways to become more aware of our spiritual sides, but there is no right or wrong way. You need to listen to the voice within you to find your spiritual side. With that being said, there are three important keys to mastering your beliefs and understanding the awesome power of spirituality that I would like to share with you. For many of us, attending to the spiritual side of ourselves starts with developing what has been described as a fear of God. In this context, fear means having reverence of or respect for God.

This should naturally progress to the second key, an awareness of God around us or what Gregg Brandon describes as the Divine Matrix in *The Divine Matrix: Bridging Time, Space, Miracles, and Belief.* The Divine Matrix is the intelligence or force that connects everything.

The third key to mastering your beliefs and realizing the power of spirituality is faith. "Without faith no one can please God. Anyone who comes to God must believe that he is real and that he rewards those who truly want to find him" (Hebrews 11:6). By pursuing these keys, we acknowledge the importance of God as the source. God is the universal intelligence that connects us to everything around us. Through faith, we can believe in what we cannot see. Our relationship with the source gives us life and makes possible all things that can happen to us—or through us. Understanding the importance of maintaining this connection to the source is fundamental to spirituality.

## Fear of God

Staying connected to the source of our power seems reasonable—and, in general, a good idea to most. Staying connected is good judgment. But more than just good judgment, staying connected to the source is essential if we are going to function at our highest potential. Like the appliances in our homes that only work the way they should if plugged into or connected to a power source, we must abide in our power source to survive, thrive, and function at peak capacity.

Fearing God is also about understanding and respecting that there are specific requirements for us to fulfill to ensure our connection to God. We must believe and behave in certain ways to remain connected. There are certain things we must be prepared to do and believe in order to maximize our relationship to the source. Compliance and obedience with these tenets is essential for demonstrating fear in God. Showing obedience shows awareness, respect, and reverence for the connecting power or force of the universe. Wise individuals fear God. Wise families, organizations, and countries fear God and show their reverence and respect by living wisely and obeying the universal laws of the force of the universe.

In *Lessons from the Richest Man Who Ever Lived*, Steve Scott speaks of the many lessons taught by King Solomon in the book of Proverbs in the Old Testament Bible. He chronicles the many benefits of wisdom that have been documented in that book. These many benefits answer the question many ask when embarking on a new practice. What are the benefits you can expect to realize by possessing a fear of God? The answer may surprise you. This fear of God translates into wisdom and wisdom brings knowledge, discretion, good judgment, fairness, preservation, protection, deliverance from your enemies, victory over your competitors, glory, longer life, honor, commendation, riches, understanding, favor with those in authority, avoidance of shame, promotions, happiness, strength, confidence, courage and extraordinary achievement, satisfaction, great relationships, a happy marriage, fulfilled and successful children, a truly meaningful life, the love and admiration of others, true wisdom, intimacy with God, and true spirituality.

To learn more about the benefits of obtaining wisdom and spirituality, I recommend that you read the book of Proverbs in the Bible as well as *Lessons from the Richest Man Who Ever Lived: Incomparable Insights, and Breakthrough Strategies for Success, Happiness, and Wealth.*

## Awareness of the Divine Matrix

The next key to spirituality is to become aware of the Divine Matrix. Braden describes the existence of a field of energy called the Divine Matrix that "provides the container as well as a bridge and a mirror, for everything that happens between the world within us and the world outside of our bodies." This field exists in everything—from the smallest particles of the quantum world to the most distant galaxies. The Matrix as described by Braden is a primal web of energy that connects our bodies, the world, and everything in the universe.

## Participatory Universe

Braden suggests that there is the possibility and likelihood that we are not just simply observers who are passing through a brief moment of time in a creation that already exists. When we look at life or our spiritual and material possessions, our relationships, careers, loves, achievements, and fears, we may also be looking in the mirror of our authentic—and sometimes unconscious—beliefs made manifest. We see them in our world because they have been made manifest through the Divine Matrix; for this to be true, consciousness must play a role in the existence of the universe. This means that we live in a participatory universe in that we—in and through our consciousness—are not only the creative art of the universe, but we are also the artists. I know that this seems unlikely, but Braden points out that this idea is at the heart of the debate between two of the greatest and most brilliant minds in recent times. Albert Einstein and John Wheeler were both Princeton physicists and colleagues who had very different views on this idea.

Braggs references a quote from Einstein's autobiographical notes that essentially illustrated his belief that we were essentially passive observers in a universe already in place. Wheeler offered a different perspective on our role in creation. He referred to the late twentieth century experiments that show us how simply looking at something changes that something. He said, "Now we learn from the quantum world that even to observe so minuscule an object as an electron we have to shatter the plate glass; we have to reach in there . . . . So the old word, observer, simply has to be crossed off the books and we must put in the new word, participatory."

This idea opens our minds to the possibility that we cannot only tell our stories from a historic perspective, but that we can also write the story so to speak as well. By the power of our consciousness, we can influence our environment and the universe. Braden's book is based on more than twenty years of research. He chronicled important experimental findings in the world of quantum physics. Not only did he review the exciting discoveries of this new science, he also explained the significance of these experiments in lay terms. Braden also proposed interpretations of these findings and the implications for how these findings change what we know about how the universe works. He indicated that the universe appears to be based on four characteristics that make things work the way they do. He believes that the key to harnessing the power of the Matrix lies in our ability to embrace four landmark discoveries that link it to our lives:

Discovery 1—There is a field of energy that connects all of creation.

Discovery 2—This field plays the role of a container, a bridge, and a mirror for the beliefs within us.

Discovery 3—The field is nonlocal and holographic. Every part of it is connected to every other—and each piece mirrors the whole on a smaller scale.

Discovery 4—We communicate with the field through the language of emotion.

Braden said that our power to recognize and apply these realities determines everything—from our healing to the success of our relationships and careers.

In the last chapter, he lists twenty keys to Conscious Creation. Three of these key findings are:

1. Human DNA has a direct effect on the stuff that our world is made of.

2. Human emotion has a direct effect on the DNA that affects the stuff that our world is made of.

3. The relationship between emotions and DNA transcends the bounds of time and space. The effects are the same—regardless of distance.

These keys—and the understanding of how they work together—will change the way you think about the universe, space, time, and your power to create. To learn more about the Matrix, read *The Divine Matrix: Bridging Time, Space, Miracles, and Belief.*

# Faith

Faith has been defined as the evidence of things hoped for and the substance of things not seen. We take the definition one step further by adding that faith is the emotional feeling and intellectual belief, without doubt, in an idea or desire of our hearts. It is also important to remember that, as the Bible tells us, faith must be accompanied by action.

> You foolish man, do you want evidence that faith without deeds is useless? Was not our ancestor Abraham considered righteous for what he did when he offered his son Isaac on the altar? You see that his faith and his actions were working together, and his faith was made complete by what he did. And the scripture

was fulfilled that says, Abraham believed God, and it was credited to him as righteousness, and he was called God's friend. You see that a person is justified by what he does and not by faith alone. (James 2:20-24, NIV).

This combination of belief without doubt—along with action consistent with that belief—is the key that makes faith perfect.

Faith means believing and demonstrating that belief with actions consistent with those beliefs. For example, if a person aspires to a goal such as to becoming a famous musician, it will be important for the person to acquire an instrument of choice, arrange to take lessons, and practice regularly. Despite the initial learning curve, faith will help the person stick to it and learn the craft. Even under the disappointment of rejection and setbacks, the faithful will not be discouraged and will not doubt their greatness. For them, it is just a matter of time. Their success is never in doubt in their minds. It is only a matter of time before they receive their big break. This person's faith and confidence in the career not yet manifested drives them to push on until everyone else realizes and appreciates what they already know by faith—the belief that he or she is an extremely special musician who will be famous soon.

This attitude of faith, anticipated success, and fulfillment can be seen in all success stories. It is this type of faith in action that moves the farmer who is praying for rain to dig irrigation ditches to collect the water that is surely on the way. Regardless of the odds or likelihood, faithful people still believe. That belief is translated into behavior and actions consistent with the outcomes hoped for. To truly have faith, we must behave as if we know, without doubt, that the outcome will occur. We must prepare for the success that we pray and hope for. We must prepare for the fulfillment of our faith. If you have faith that you will purchase the home you always wanted, make an appointment with a real estate agent in the area you want to live, research mortgage rates with several banks, and decide what neighborhood you want to live in. If you are praying for a second car, clean out the garage so you can have a place to park the new one. Plan to have what you hope and pray for. Expect to receive what you desire. See it, feel it, and anticipate it in every way. Think about how you will feel when you acquire what you are hoping for. Act as if you have it and reflect on that feeling regularly. Without any doubt, believe and you will receive what your heart desires. It is yours to create in your mind. The power of your mind will make it so.

# Seven: Master Your Mind—The Power of Thinking

"As a man thinketh in his heart, so is he" (Proverbs 23:7).

Mastering the mind and thinking is certainly one of the most important steps to success and achieving the extraordinary life you want. Everything starts in the mind as it did in the very beginning. The mind of God or universal intelligence was the source of the Word. Words are thoughts. These words or thought images are the stuff that everything is made of. Before anything can be or exist, it must first exist as a thought or word.

"In the beginning was the Word, and the Word was with God and the Word was God. The same was in the beginning with God. All things were made by him; and without him was not anything made that was made" John 1:13.

Thoughts are the key to creation. What we think about determines what we will do, experience, and create for ourselves in life. This is a powerful idea—and it is as true for good thoughts that we wish for ourselves as it is for bad thoughts that we wish to avoid. What we allow our minds to dwell upon with thoughts will be created. Thoughts are what everything is made of. Everything from the beginning originated as first a thought. The chair you are sitting on and the paper or electronic device you are now reading from was first a thought in someone's mind. Those thoughts were made manifest and the result is what you see. Thoughts are the stuff that dreams are made of. The key to realizing your dreams and deepest desires is to use your thoughts to create your desired reality. This sounds easy, but it could be challenging for someone who does not have a good working knowledge of the mind and the media of the mind, thoughts.

Our minds are our most powerful asset. It is the most powerful tool known to man. It is the most powerful tool, period. Yet in our modern day society very little, if any, time is spent teaching people about how to use their minds. We seldom receive any instruction on how to use the reticular activating system, conscious, subconscious, and super conscious mind. Most people only understand their conscious mind—the part that we use when we think while in the conscious state. By not engaging the power of the subconscious mind, many fail to realize the utility of the most powerful tool available.

Since thoughts flow through our minds like a never-ending stream of water, we are almost constantly feeding the subconscious with instructions. The mind is a conduit for a constant stream of consciousness that flows and carries thoughts of memories, ideas, emotions, expectations, beliefs, desires, and more. Because of this constant flow of thoughts or instructions, it is important to develop skills to control the quality and character of thoughts flowing through our minds.

Since the subconscious is working with the reticular activating system to create and attract whatever is being thought about, we need to make sure that our thoughts are congruent with our intentions, desires, expectations, plans, and actions. The use of meditation could be a great tool to help quiet the flow of thoughts and help refine the quality and character of your thoughts to ensure congruency between what you want and what you think. There are a number of audio products that can help you get started with meditations if you do not have any experience meditating. I recommend *Creative Visualization Meditations* by Shakti Gawain and *The Secret Universal Mind Meditation* and *Secret Universal Mind Meditations II* by Kelly Howell.

The conscious part of our minds accounts for only a small amount of our mental capacity. Dealing only with this aspect of your mind limits your ability to actively engage and leverage the more powerful parts of your mind: the subconscious and super-conscious. There are ways to better use your mind to help create what you want. This starts with learning the importance of controlling the nature and quality of thoughts that pass through our minds.

Since we create what we think, it is important to think of what we want. Intellectual discipline is required to ensure productive control of thoughts. Thoughts that positively support what is desired will create the desired reality. Individuals that fail to control their thoughts in a positive way and may find themselves thinking of what they do not want more than anything else. Mental focus on what is not desired or what is feared will attract and create circumstances that are not desired. This also works for the words that we use.

Remember that words are thoughts written down or spoken. Words and thoughts have power. This power can create what you want or manifest your greatest fears. A negative cliché often will become true for the person who speaks it into reality. "We can't catch a break" or "With our luck, something bad will happen" become a self-fulfilling prophecy for the millions of people who engage in what I call self-limiting subconscious programming.

It is also important to know that the subconscious takes our thoughts and words literally and does not recognize words like "not." When a person says or thinks that they do not want to be in debt, their subconscious minds only hear the words, "want to be in debt." As a result, they create more debt for themselves. "I do not want to be late for my meeting" is heard by the subconscious as, "I want to be late." To prevent this negative programming, practice taking notices of your thoughts and words over the next few days and change your phraseology to result in positive programming. Instead of saying, "I don't want to have an accident or get a ticket on this road trip," you should say, think, and or pray the positive version of this idea. You should rephrase the words to something like, "I want to have a safe and pleasant trip." This rephrasing will change the results you get and will change your life.

There are a few key principles that will help you master your mind through right thinking:

1. Think positive thoughts

2. Expect positive outcomes

3. Act as if the thought has been fulfilled

4. Use meditation and affirmations to reprogram the subconscious

5. Believe and feel the outcome achieved

6. Enjoy an attitude of gratitude

These basic principles—when practiced with congruency—will ensure right thinking. Right thinking will allow you to become the creator of your own future. The thoughts you think today are the seeds that will form your reality and life tomorrow. You are always creating with your mind—whether you realize it or not. You are the artist. Paint or sculpt the world you want. In this universe, you possess the power within your mind to do what you make up your mind to do. The key is to apply these principles consistently and to have the discipline to make sure that you maintain the highest levels of congruency between your thoughts, actions, feelings, and beliefs. It is also important not to press or stress over what you want. The universe seems to have a way to sensing the full-court press. This has the opposite effect.

Be willing to just let it go and do not worry about the outcome. Don't worry about when or how it will happen—just maintain a quiet confidence that it is as good as done. Live your life now with the satisfaction of knowing that your dreams are reality. Universal intelligence will find a way to attract the life you want.

*The Power of the Body, Mind, and Spirit: 7 Keys to Creating the Life You Want Now*—a seven-step guide to success and the extraordinary life you want—is based on universal truth. I hope you take the time to explore the other readings and ideas that I have suggested. These ideas will serve as the key to open up unlimited possibilities for your life. You are the artist—make a commitment to practice the seven steps daily. This will allow you to paint or sculpt the life you think, see, feel, and believe. Stop talking about it and take action daily and it will be yours. Remember it all starts with deciding what you want. Make a long list of what you want. Do not limit yourself. Dream big and be true to yourself. Then change what you do. Different actions will yield different results. Prepare to receive it. See, hear, and feel it as if it is done. The more vivid your visualizations are, the more powerfully your desires will be attracted to you.

Commit to mastering your body, emotions, and beliefs—and then master the awesome power of your mind. Think right thoughts, reprogram your subconscious mind, and unleash the power within you. Remember to be grateful for what you have and enjoy the journey that is your life. Thank you.

# References

1. Matthew 21:22 (King James Version)

2. Psalms 37:4-5 (King James Version)

3. Vitale, Joe. 2007. The Missing Secret, How to use the Law of Attraction to Easily Attract What You Want . . . Ever Time. Simon and Schuster Audio, Hypnotic Marketing, Inc., Nightingale-Conant Corporation.

4. Tracy, Brian. 1997. The Luck Factor, How to Take the Chance Out of Becoming a Success. Nightingale-Conant Corporation.

5. Canfield, Jack. 1989, 2002. Maximum Confidence, 10 Secrets of Extreme Self-Esteem. Simon and Schuster Audio, Nightingale Conant Corporation.

6. Collier, Robert. The Secret of the Ages. Wildside Press.

7. St. Johns, Noah. 2007. The Great Little Book of Afformations. Gildan Media Corporation.

8. John 1:1-3 (King James Version)

9. Gawain, Shakti. 1978. Creative Visualization Meditations. MJF Books.

10. Strozzi-Heckler, Richard. 2003. Being Human at Work: Bringing Somatic Intelligence into Your Professional Life. North Atlantic Books.

11. Strozzi-Heckler, Richard. 2007. The Leadership Dojo. Frog Books.

12. Mehrabian, Albert. 1971. Silent Messages. Wadsworth Publishing Company.

13. Davidson, Alan. 2010. Body Brilliance: Mastering Your Five Vital Intelligences. Elite Books.

14. Franklin, Jentezen, 2007. Fasting. Charisma House.

15. Ecclesiastes 4:12 (King James Version)

16. Matthew 17:20-21 (King James Version)

17. Exodus 34: 27-28 (King James Version)

18. Esther 4:7

19. Rogers, Bob. 1995. 101 Reasons to Fast. Bob Rodgers Ministries.

20. Matthew 6:33 (King James Version)

21. Manz, Charles. 2003. Emotional Discipline: The Power to Choose How You Feel, 5 Life Changing Steps to Feel Better Every Day. Berrett-Koehler.

22. Gregg, Branden. 2008. The Divine Matrix, Bridging Time, Space, Miracles, and Belief. Hay House.

23. Hebrews 11:6 (King James Version)

24. Scott, Steve. 2006. Lessons From the Richest Man Who Ever Lived. Crown Business.

25. James 2:20-24 (New International Version)

26. Proverbs 23:7 (King James Version)

27. John 1:13 (King James Version)

28. Howell, Kelly. 2006. The Secret Universal Mind Meditation. Brain Sync.

CPSIA information can be obtained at www.ICGtesting.com
Printed in the USA
BVOW060818040512

289238BV00005B/1/P